FRANCIS FRITH'S

WOLVERHAMPTON

PHOTOGRAPHIC MEMORIES

DAVID CLARE works at the University of Wolverhampton in the Department of Learning Resources. He went to University at Lampeter and Sheffield. He has lived in Wolverhampton all his life and is an acknowledged local expert on the buildings and history of Wolverhampton.

FRANCIS FRITH'S
PHOTOGRAPHIC MEMORIES

WOLVERHAMPTON

PHOTOGRAPHIC MEMORIES

DAVID CLARE

First published in the United Kingdom in 2005 by
The Francis Frith Collection®

Limited hardback edition published in 2005 ISBN 1-84589-021-3

Paperback edition 2005 ISBN 1-85937-970-2

British Library Cataloguing in Publication Data

Wolverhampton - Photographic Memories
David Clare

The Francis Frith Collection
Frith's Barn, Teffont,
Salisbury, Wiltshire SP3 5QP
Tel: +44 (0) 1722 716 376
Email: info@francisfrith.co.uk
www.francisfrith.co.uk

Printed and bound in Great Britain

Front Cover: **WOLVERHAMPTON,** *Lichfield Street c1955* W285010t
Frontispiece: **WOLVERHAMPTON,** *St Peter's Gardens and Barclays Bank
c1955,* W285305

*The colour-tinting is for illustrative purposes only, and is not intended
to be historically accurate*

Aerial photographs reproduced under licence from Simmons Aerofilms Limited.
Historical Ordnance Survey maps reproduced under licence from Homecheck.co.uk

The author and publisher gratefully acknowledge the assistance of the following in
providing extra material for use in this book:
Wolverhampton Wanderers Football Club Archives, Peter Harrington LBIPP, Wolves
official photographer, Graham Hughes, Wolves historian.

CONTENTS

FRANCIS FRITH
VICTORIAN PIONEER

FRANCIS FRITH, founder of the world-famous photographic archive, was a complex and multi-talented man. A devout Quaker and a highly successful Victorian businessman, he was philo-sophical by nature and pioneering in outlook.

By 1855 he had already established a wholesale grocery business in Liverpool, and sold it for the astonishing sum of £200,000, which is the equivalent today of over £15,000,000. Now a very rich man, he was able to indulge his passion for travel. As a child he had pored over travel books written by early explorers, and his fancy and imagination had been stirred by family holi-days to the sublime mountain regions of Wales and Scotland. 'What lands of spirit-stirring and enriching scenes and places!' he had written. He was to return to these scenes of grandeur in later years to 'recapture the thousands of vivid and tender memories', but with a different pur-pose. Now in his thirties, and captivated by the new science of photography, Frith set out on a series of pioneering journeys up the Nile and

to the Near East that occupied him from 1856 until 1860.

INTRIGUE AND EXPLORATION

These far-flung journeys were packed with intrigue and adventure. In his life story, writ-ten when he was sixty-three, Frith tells of being held captive by bandits, and of fighting 'an awful midnight battle to the very point of surrender with a deadly pack of hungry, wild dogs'. Wearing flowing Arab costume, Frith arrived at Akaba by camel sixty years before Lawrence of Arabia, where he encountered 'desert princes and rival sheikhs, blazing with jewel-hilted swords'.

He was the first photographer to venture beyond the sixth cataract of the Nile. Africa was still the mysterious 'Dark Continent', and Stanley and Livingstone's historic meeting was a decade into the future. The conditions for picture tak-ing confound belief. He laboured for hours in his wicker dark-room in the sweltering heat of the desert, while the volatile chemicals fizzed dangerously in their trays. Back in London he exhibited his photographs and was 'rapturously cheered' by members of the Royal Society. His reputation as a photographer was made over-night.

VENTURE OF A LIFE-TIME

Characteristically, Frith quickly spotted the opportunity to create a new business as a spe-cialist publisher of photographs. He lived in an era of immense and sometimes violent change.

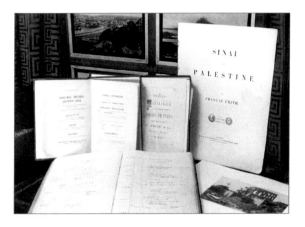

For the poor in the early part of Victoria's reign work was exhausting and the hours long, and people had precious little free time to enjoy themselves. Most had no transport other than a cart or gig at their disposal, and rarely travelled far beyond the boundaries of their own town or village. However, by the 1870s the railways had threaded their way across the country, and Bank Holidays and half-day Saturdays had been made obligatory by Act of Parliament. All of a sudden the working man and his family were able to enjoy days out and see a little more of the world.

With typical business acumen, Francis Frith foresaw that these new tourists would enjoy having souvenirs to commemorate their days out. In 1860 he married Mary Ann Rosling and set out on a new career: his aim was to photograph every city, town and village in Britain. For the next thirty years he travelled the country by train and by pony and trap, producing fine photographs of seaside resorts and beauty spots that were keenly bought by millions of Victorians. These prints were painstakingly pasted into family albums and pored over during the dark nights of winter, rekindling precious memories of summer excursions.

THE RISE OF FRITH & CO

Frith's studio was soon supplying retail shops all over the country. To meet the demand he gathered about him a small team of photographers, and published the work of independent artist-photographers of the calibre of Roger Fenton and Francis Bedford. In order to gain some understanding of the scale of Frith's business one only has to look at the catalogue issued by Frith & Co in 1886: it runs to some 670 pages, listing not only many thousands of views of the British Isles but also many photographs of most European countries, and China, Japan, the USA and Canada - note the sample page shown on page 9 from the hand-written Frith & Co ledgers recording the pictures. By 1890 Frith had created the greatest specialist photographic publishing company in the world, with over 2,000 sales outlets - more than the combined number that Boots and WH Smith have today! The picture on the next page shows the Frith & Co display board at Ingleton in the Yorkshire Dales (left of window). Beautifully constructed with a mahogany frame and gilt inserts, it could display up to a dozen local scenes.

POSTCARD BONANZA

The ever-popular holiday postcard we know today took many years to develop. In 1870 the Post Office issued the first plain cards, with a pre-printed stamp on one face. In 1894 they allowed other publishers' cards to be sent through the mail with an attached adhesive halfpenny stamp. Demand grew rapidly, and in 1895 a new size of postcard was permitted called the court card, but there was little room for illustration. In 1899, a year after Frith's death, a new card measuring 5.5 x 3.5 inches became the standard format, but it was not until 1902 that the divided back came into being, so that the address and message could be on one face and a full-size illustration on the other. Frith & Co were in the vanguard of postcard development: Frith's sons Eustace and Cyril continued their father's monumental task, expanding the number of views offered to the public and recording more and more places

in Britain, as the coasts and countryside were opened up to mass travel.

Francis Frith had died in 1898 at his villa in Cannes, his great project still growing. The archive he created continued in business for another seventy years. By 1970 it contained over a third of a million pictures showing 7,000 British towns and villages.

FRANCIS FRITH'S LEGACY

Frith's legacy to us today is of immense significance and value, for the magnificent archive of evocative photographs he created provides a unique record of change in the cities, towns and villages throughout Britain over a century and more. Frith and his fellow studio photographers revisited locations many times down the years to update their views, compiling for us an enthralling and colourful pageant of British life and character.

We are fortunate that Frith was dedicated to recording the minutiae of everyday life, for it is this sheer wealth of visual data, the painstaking chronicle of changes in dress, transport, street layouts, buildings, housing, engineering and landscape that captivates us so much today. His remarkable images offer us a powerful link with the past and with the lives of our ancestors.

THE VALUE OF THE ARCHIVE TODAY

Computers have now made it possible for Frith's many thousands of images to be accessed almost instantly. Frith's images are increasingly used as visual resources, by social historians, by researchers into genealogy and ancestry, by architects and town planners, and by teachers involved in local history projects.

In addition, the archive offers every one of us an opportunity to examine the places where we and our families have lived and worked down the years. Highly successful in Frith's own era, the archive is now, a century and more on, entering a new phase of popularity. Historians consider the Francis Frith Collection to be of prime national importance. It is the only archive of its kind remaining in private ownership. Francis Frith's archive is now housed in an historic timber barn in the beautiful village of Teffont in Wiltshire. Its founder would not recognize the archive office as it is today. In place of the many thousands of dusty boxes containing glass plate negatives and an all-pervading odour of photographic chemicals, there are now ranks of computer screens. He would be amazed to watch his images travelling round the world at unimaginable speeds through internet lines.

The archive's future is both bright and exciting. Francis Frith, with his unshakeable belief in making photographs available to the greatest number of people, would undoubtedly approve of what is being done today with his lifetime's work. His photographs depicting our shared past are now bringing pleasure and enlightenment to millions around the world a century and more after his death.

WOLVERHAMPTON
AN INTRODUCTION

HEATED ARGUMENTS rage about whether Wolverhampton is in or out of the Black Country. In fact the city lies squarely across the north-west border of the region and was historically in Staffordshire. Residents in the leafy western suburbs some years ago were surprised to see new signs on the main roads welcoming them to the Black Country. The inhabitants of the industrial eastern suburbs on the other hand are amazed that anyone could imagine that they were not part of the Black Country.

There are two Wolverhamptons. One matches the prevailing national image of a dull, uninteresting, unattractive industrial city with nothing worthy of distinction other than Wolverhampton Wanderers Football Club. The other Wolverhampton is the one that Wulfrunians know: a city with a distinct and thriving shopping centre, with miles of quiet green suburbs and distinct local village or town centres such as Penn, Tettenhall, Bilston and Wednesfield. Wulfrunians have all the advantages of living in the West Midland conurbation with the bonus of never being more than two or three miles from unspoiled open countryside.

The local accent is distinct from that of neighbours such as Sedgley, Dudley, Tipton and Birmingham, most of all Birmingham. The Wolverhampton accent is sadly not highly regarded nationally and is lumped together with all West Midland accents as Brummie. Nothing annoys Wolverhampton folk more than to be labelled Brummies by their accent. In fact they would not live in Birmingham if they had the choice, and they pity those who do.

The list of famous people coming from Wolverhampton is not a long one, consisting largely of modern sportsmen and women and popular singers. The most successful pop acts are Slade and Beverley Knight. However Dame Maggie Teyte, the early 20th-century international soprano, was also born in Wolverhampton. The town also attained some notoriety in the 1960s when the local MP Enoch Powell made his famous speech on immigration predicting dire consequences if it was not controlled.

This book is not a history of Wolverhampton

but it is appropriate to give some background to the pictures. Wolverhampton was a town, and is now a city, that began as an Anglo-Saxon settlement well before the Domesday survey of 1086. Some of the place names in the area are Celtic: Penn (hill, top), Trysull Brook, now the Smestow Brook, (from 'troi', the Celtic word for turn, twist), but no evidence of a pre-Anglo-Saxon settlement at Wolverhampton has been found. Let us at this point dispose of the myth, recently become more widespread, that the Mercian king Wulfhere founded the town in the 7th century. There is no evidence for this apart from a fanciful derivation of the name of the town. The traditional foundation date is AD985, when Aethelred granted land at Heantune to Lady Wulfruna, but this suggests there already was a settlement. She endowed the church in 994. Incidentally I have deliberately used the word town when referring to Wolverhampton before 2000, and the word city for subsequent years.

After the Conquest of 1066 the Norman barons were given control of all England by the new king, William I, who gave to Samson of Bayeux the lands of Hantone (High town), together with the slaves, villagers and other inhabitants, who would have carried on their lives much as before, not caring which particular lord they served.

In medieval times the town was a centre of the wool trade, hence the woolsack in its coat of arms.

Wolverhampton has featured remarkably little in national upheavals over its 1000 years. After the Gunpowder Plot of 1605, some of the conspirators were chased to nearby Holbeach House at Himley. The town was very active in the 1640s during the English Civil War. In 1642 Prince Rupert passed through the town, stopping at a house in Victoria Street. Important local families supported the king, so Wolverhampton was a Royalist town if anything, but it fell without resistance to the Parliamentarians in 1643. King Charles I came through in 1645 and stayed overnight. The fleeing King Charles II stayed at Moseley Old Hall and hid in the oak tree at

WOLVERHAMPTON *c1890* W285303

11

Boscobel, and the restoration of the monarchy was declared on High Green (Queen Square) in 1660, but that was all the excitement there was going to be.

Little of medieval, Tudor and 17th-century Wolverhampton survives today. We can still see the churches in the city centre and at Penn, Bushbury and Tettenhall, a half-timbered remnant in Victoria Street, another in Exchange Street and a few scattered farm buildings, for example at Northicote and Merridale. The basic street plan however survives remarkably well. In the city centre the modern streets generally overlie their medieval counterparts. Former places such as High Green (Queen Square), Cock Street (Victoria Street), Horse Fair (Wulfruna Street), Goat or Tup Street (North Street) and Barn Street (Salop Street) have all been renamed, but Dudley Street, Lichfield Street and Stafford Street still bear their old names. Old photographs and engravings show some of the buildings that have been lost. There was a fine Tudor hall in Queen Square, demolished in 1841. Lichfield Street was lined with half-timbered buildings until all were cleared away in the 1880s to widen the street and build the Art Gallery. The building on the corner where Barclays Bank now stands was a particularly fine example of 16th-century architecture that lasted until the 1870s. The town centre was largely rebuilt in the 19th century and much Victorian architecture remains in several main streets, but Dudley Street and Victoria Street, the two main shopping areas, consist of more modern buildings with very few exceptions. The photographs in this book of Queen Square, the area round the Art Gallery and down Lichfield Street to the Britannia Hotel are still very recognizable today. Most of the buildings look cleaner and in better repair now than they did 50 years ago. Other pictures will be familiar to older inhabitants but strange to the young. The area around Molineux and down North Street for example has completely changed since the 1970s. Although much enlarged by many new houses, Tettenhall and Penn are still highly sought-after residential districts, while Bilston and Wednesfield have benefited from bypasses, but retain much of their character.

WOLVERHAMPTON, *New Market Hall c1965* W285056

The industrial revolution that began in Shropshire came to Wolverhampton, a quiet little market town, and completely transformed it. The population grew from 12,000 in 1801, to 50,000 by 1851, 100,000 by 1921 and nearly 250,000 today, with the inclusion of Bilston, Tettenhall and Wednesfield. The population has been greater than this since the war, but the replacement of many of the streets of small terraced houses by modern houses at a lower density has meant that fewer people live inside the city boundaries. The 19th century saw the rapid building of much needed housing, which for the ordinary worker was largely cheap and crowded, although many better houses were built for the middle classes. Wolverhampton has had its borders drawn very tightly around the existing built-up areas, so much expansion has had to take place just outside the borough boundaries in Staffordshire, in Perton and Wombourne.

Wolverhampton's industries in the 19th century ranged from japanned ware, lock manufacture, tin ware, steel products, chemical works, brewing, iron foundries and brassware, to hundreds of small manufacturing businesses making everything the consumer needed. Wolverhampton was ideally placed to benefit from the proximity of raw materials and good transport connections by road and canal, and later rail. 100 years ago the town was described by some as being without trees and greenery, a real part of the Black Country, and by others as being elevated, airy and surrounded by lovely countryside. This conflict of images of the city is still the same today. Industrial development continued through the 20th century as Wolverhampton added other industries such as vehicle and engine manufacture to its industrial base.

After the demolition of whole districts in the 1950s, 60s and 70s for redevelopment and to construct the ring road, local planners realised almost too late that they still had much of interest and attractiveness worth preserving in the city. A process of preservation and regeneration began which has included restoration work on Lindy Lou and the upper floor of the building next door in Victoria Street, shops in Lichfield Passage and Worcester Street, terraces of 18th-century buildings in King Street, George Street and Snow Hill, and St Peter's Gardens. There are other examples around the city of similar efforts to rescue its architectural heritage. Parallel with this has been the drive to put residential accommodation back into the city centre. In common with many places, by the 1990s, the centre of Wolverhampton had become a place in which no-one would choose to live. In the last ten years upper floors of shops have been renovated to become apartments, and prestige city centre homes have appeared in Market Square, by the canal in Horseley Field and elsewhere.

Wolverhampton is unfortunate in lacking an outer ring road. The roads into the city are generally wide and do their job well but through traffic going from north to south and east to west has to go almost into the centre to get round the city, take an enormous detour, or suffer the clogged M6. The M54 and Black Country Route have helped a little, as has the new toll motorway, but it is a pity that no-one had the foresight in the 1930s to plan a route around the perimeter of the town. To build such a route would nowadays be very expensive and disruptive of residential areas and the proposed construction of a route further out into the countryside, such as the currently abandoned western bypass, has been understandably bitterly fought against by people who moved out there for some peace and quiet.

In the old photographs in this book we can see the story of our times and the changes that have happened over the years. Until recently scant regard was paid to preserving the heritage of the buildings all around us, especially in a city like Wolverhampton, which was not regarded as being of great architectural interest. Fortunately we now live in an age when old buildings are valued for giving us continuity with our past, and a good quality of urban environment is recognised as an asset in our daily lives. We all feel better for living in an attractive and well looked after place. It is also the case that prosperity attracts prosperity and the downward economic slide of a town is worsened by obvious signs of urban blight. Whatever our political views might be, it is unarguable that Wolverhampton today is a cleaner, brighter and better cared-for place than it has been for a long time.

WOLVERHAMPTON, *Dudley Street c1900* W285007

QUEEN SQUARE
AND LICHFIELD STREET

THIS IS THE OLD HEART of the city, the centre of the spider's web of roads that run in all directions from the square and from nearby St Peter's Church to the neighbouring towns of Stafford, Lichfield, Walsall, Dudley, Worcester and Bridgnorth. The square itself was the original market place, High Green, with stalls, butchers' shambles, corn market, charity school, the Tudor High Hall, home of the Levesons, and the Town Hall of 1687.

Originally a mainly half-timbered town in the midland tradition, Wolverhampton has seen its old buildings replaced over the years with Georgian brick, and then Victorian brick, terracotta and stone. Luckily the replacement and rebuilding process in Queen Square and Lichfield Street was halted in the 20th century just in time to preserve most of the Victorian townscape, which has now been cleaned and restored to good appearance.

Plans for improving Queen Square will enhance its attractiveness and reclaim more of it for the pedestrian, which can only be a good thing.

WOLVERHAMPTON, *Queen Square 1890* W285006

Next to the shop behind the wicker cart is the Empire Music Hall, which became the Empire Palace Theatre in 1898. The Café Royal in the centre has lost a storey and is now HSBC Bank. Next to it are two elegant Georgian houses soon to be replaced in the early 1900s by the Queen's Ballroom and then by a clumsy addition to Lloyds bank.

WOLVERHAMPTON
Queen Square 1910
W285002

The Empire Palace, opened in 1898, became the Hippodrome in 1921. Burned out in 1956 it was replaced by Times Furnishing, then Yates's Wine Lodge. Harley's is on part of the site of Harley's Wine Vaults, removed when this end of the square was widened. Queen's Arcade on the right smoothly continues the line of Victorian buildings round into Victoria Street.

WOLVERHAMPTON, *Queen Square c1900* ZZZ03806 (Author's Collection)

This side of Queen Square has not changed very much in 100 years. Harmer's Home Brewed Ales are on sale at the Board, which has now been replaced by a mock Tudor black and white building. The flamboyant advertisement for Craddock's Shoes would not be allowed today. A fire appliance waits by Prince Albert's statue for an emergency.

◄ **WOLVERHAMPTON**
Queen Square c1910
ZZZ03807 (Author's
Collection)

An open-topped tram makes its way down Queen Square to turn left into Victoria Street. Queen's Arcade on the right opened in 1910 and had another, smaller, entrance in Victoria Street. This graceful corner is no more. There is now an ugly concrete minor entrance to the Mander Centre, which is only two storeys high and out of scale with the rest of the square.

WOLVERHAMPTON

Queen Square c1920 ZZZ03808 (Author's Collection)

Hemming's, Altham's and Cope's Wine Lodge still look out today over Queen Square but the buildings have different occupants. Cope's was originally a 16th-century half-timbered building, refaced with a Georgian brick frontage in 1726 to modernise it. Part of the rear off Exchange Street is still half-timbered. It has recently been well restored as a branch of the Staffordshire building society.

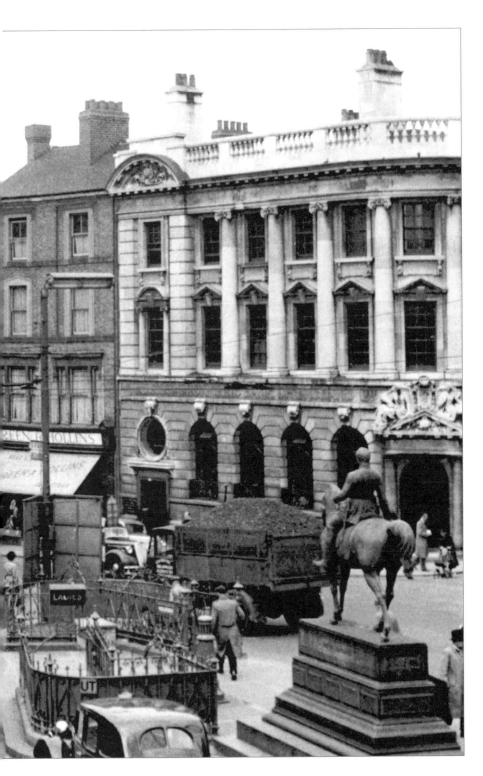

WOLVERHAMPTON
Queen Square c1955
W285013
Prince Albert has looked down Darlington Street to St Mark's Church since 1866 and has been moved several times over the years. The railings guard the steps to the sadly missed underground public conveniences. The coal lorry, a rare sight nowadays, is passing a branch of the National Provincial Bank of England of c1905. Green and Hollins is now a bank.

21

▼ **WOLVERHAMPTON,** *Queen Square c1960* W285048

The ancient market place of the town was called High Green until renamed Queen Square in 1866 on the visit of Queen Victoria. Most of the banks had their main branches here: going round the square from the left, Martin's Bank, National Provincial Bank, Barclays Bank on the corner of Lichfield street, Midland Bank on the opposite corner and Lloyds Bank just visible next to the Queen's Ballroom.

► **WOLVERHAMPTON**
Lichfield Street c1905
ZZZ03809 (Author's Collection)

This end of Lichfield Street from Victoria Square to Prince's Square was built as a new street to the railway station in the 1880s and 1890s. The buildings on the right were replaced in the 1930s by a modern Co-op department store. 'When Knights Were Bold' is on at the Grand Theatre.

WOLVERHAMPTON
Lichfield Street
c1955 W285010

The Grand Theatre, designed by C J Phipps, a well-known theatrical architect, opened in 1894. It was always Wolverhampton's proper dramatic theatre – the others offered variety. The Co-op van waits outside the main Co-op store in the town, an ambitious 1930s building, now used as bars. The Royal London Insurance building at the end of the street is now shops, bars and private apartments.

▶ **WOLVERHAMPTON**
Lichfield Street c1905
W285004

The view east down the street from Barclays Bank is fortunately still familiar. Apart from the Midland Bank, rebuilt in 1910, only the shop names have changed. The little boy standing between the tramlines looking at the car is quite safe. Cars were still unusual enough to pose little danger and to be objects of curiosity. The car's number plate is DA44, an early Wolverhampton registration.

WOLVERHAMPTON
Lichfield Street c1955
W285011

As the street approaches
Queen Square the buildings
become more and more
imposing. Dating from
the widening of the street
in the 1870s and 1880s,
from the right they are: the
Royal London building of
1902, the Midland Bank
of 1910, the Art Gallery of
1883-5, and Barclays Bank
of 1876. The picture looks
dated because of the old-
fashioned bollards and
street signs.

WOLVERHAMPTON, *St Peter's Gardens and the Art Gallery c1955* W285304

The splendid Art Gallery was largely paid for by the builder Philip Horseman, who also presented the fountain to the town. The rear part of the Art Gallery was for many years part of the College of Art. The gardens were laid out after the medieval shops in Lichfield Street were demolished in the 1880s.

◄ **WOLVERHAMPTON** *St Peter's Gardens and Barclays Bank c1955* W285305

The gardens lost their distinctive Victorian railings to the wartime metal salvage effort when most houses in the town had their ironwork roughly torn out, causing damage still to be seen. The railings have recently been replaced to a design as close to the original as possible. Barclays Bank is now stripped of its foliage.

WOLVERHAMPTON
Lichfield Street and the Art Gallery c1955 W285012

This view is different now because the street is a major bus route, and car traffic is generally not allowed. Otherwise the Art Gallery has watched over the same street scene for well over a century. It was designed by Julius Chatwin of Birmingham in Italianate style. The former Midland Bank next door is now a night-club called the Bank.

WOLVERHAMPTON
from the air 1937 AF53724

ST PETER'S CHURCH AND THE SURROUNDING AREA

SIGNS AROUND St Peter's Gardens describe this as the oldest part of Wolverhampton and it is difficult to argue otherwise. In medieval times St Peter's Church, perched up on the ridge, would have been surrounded by a huddle of buildings and the oldest photographs show that there was a row of medieval buildings in Lichfield Street where the gardens are now. There is an old building-height restriction in force around the church so that it can never be dominated by its neighbours. Thanks to this and its prominent location the church can be seen from many miles away, especially from the west, when the reddish sandstone of the west front glows from the warm light of the setting sun on summer evenings.

Just behind it was The Horsefair, a street leading down to North Street by Giffard House, and the Deanery, a striking 17th-century building supposed by some to have been designed by Sir Christopher Wren, which was demolished in 1931 when the College of Technology was built.

WOLVERHAMPTON, *St Peter's Church c1955* W285503

The 9th-century Saxon pillar on the left was carved with intricate animal designs but 1000 years of weather and pollution have obliterated most of the detail. St Peter's tower and nave date from the 15th century. In the 19th century restoration the incongruous chancel built in the 17th century was replaced by the more sympathetic chancel we see today.

WOLVERHAMPTON
St Peter's Church c1960
W285047

Wolverhampton's parish church was originally dedicated to St Mary and was endowed by Lady Wulfruna. This is how Wolverhampton got its name - Wulfrun Heantun (High Town). The present church was built of sandstone quarried from the rock on which it stands. It was heavily restored in the 19th century.

WOLVERHAMPTON
The Market 1910
W285008

St Peter's Church looks out over a busy market day scene next to the Market Hall, which was built in 1853. In 1961 both the open and closed markets were moved across town to the present site in School Street. All the land in the foreground became a public car park, and then the site of the Civic Centre, built in 1974.

WOLVERHAMPTON
The Market Place and St Peter's Church c1955
W285015

This is not a market day. The cars are parked where the stalls will be put up. This site and the lower part of Wulfruna Street on the left are now buried under the Civic Centre. The overhead wires remind us that trolleybuses came down this street and turned into North Street at the bottom on their way to Fordhouses.

WOLVERHAMPTON, *St Peter's Square 1974* ZZZ03810 (Author's Collection)

St Peter's Church Hall stands in the centre between the trees of St Peter's School playground and the Polytechnic building on the corner. The Hall, School and trees were all cleared to make way for the new Polytechnic buildings in 1976. The University has recently extended its buildings in this street to enlarge the Learning Centre.

WOLVERHAMPTON
Technical College,
Wulfruna Street
c1935 ZZZ03811
(Author's Collection)

The main block of the
Technical College, later
the Polytechnic and
now the University, was
constructed in 1932.
Now the University
has more than 20,000
students from all over
the world. The 17th-
century Deanery stood
on this site and panelling
from its Oak Room was
preserved and installed
in the new building.

WOLVERHAMPTON, *The Civic Centre Site 1974* ZZZ03812 (Author's Collection)

Seen from St Peter's church tower, the site of the car park and the Wholesale Market has been cleared to allow the Civic
Centre to be built. Giffard House and the Molineux Hotel on the right used to be in the same street. The Civic Centre
took several years to build as the foundations were excavated down into the sandstone bedrock to accommodate an
underground car park. It won a Civic Trust Award.

WOLVERHAMPTON
The Wholesale Market,
Wulfruna Street 1973
ZZZ03813 (Author's Collection)

Designed by J W Bradley, the
Wholesale Market was an
imposing brick and terracotta
building opened in 1903.
It stood on one side of the
continuation of Wulfruna
Street down to North Street
by Giffard House. At the
back of the building were
the Municipal Cold Stores.
Everything was demolished
in 1973 to put up the Civic
Centre complex.

THE SHOPPING AREAS

THE MAIN SHOPPING AREA is approximately enclosed by Queen Square to the north, Dudley Street to the east, Victoria Street to the west and Cleveland Street to the south. Obviously the shops extend much more widely than this but the prime sites lie within these boundaries.

20th-century street widening and rebuilding over the centuries have spared very few of the old buildings, some of which nonetheless managed to last until the 1960s and 1970s before being demolished. However the character of these streets now comes from their bustling atmosphere, which is noticeable also in the oldest photographs in this collection. The massive Mander Centre and Wulfrun Centre of the 1960s and 1970s fill almost the entire centre of the area, but do it without ruining the street scene. Pedestrian access to the shopping precincts is made through a variety of modestly sized entrances, walkways right through some large stores and several old alleyways. Vehicle and service access is wisely kept out of the main pedestrian zones.

Plans on the drawing board envisage extending the main shopping zone considerably to the south to link up with the markets and the St John's Urban Village regeneration area. Wisely the plans include preserving the best old buildings in the development zone.

WOLVERHAMPTON, *Dudley Street c1900* W285007

The busiest shopping street in the city, Dudley Street has been rebuilt continually since medieval times. Names recognizable here are H Samuel and Freeman Hardy and Willis. After being choked with cars until the 1970s, the street is now a pedestrianised zone. One difference from today's street scene is that everyone here is wearing a hat, even the children.

WOLVERHAMPTON
*Central Arcade, Dudley
Street 1973* ZZZ03814
(Author's Collection)

This is now the Dudley Street
entrance to the Mander Centre.
The brick and terracotta
Central Arcade opened in 1905,
and originally went through
to John Street, almost into
Victoria Street. There was a
musicians' gallery from which
a small orchestra entertained.
It was foreshortened when
the Mander Centre was built
but this entrance, and the
uniformly fronted shops inside,
survived until a fire finished
them off in 1974 just before
they were due to be restored.

◄ **WOLVERHAMPTON**
Dudley Street c1955
W285009

With few families able to afford cars, parking was easy in the 1950s. Dolcis Shoes is a long established business but all of the shops in view at the bottom of the street were demolished in the 1960s to allow the Wulfrun Centre to be built. The central arcade was just beyond the lamp-post in the centre of the photograph.

◄ **WOLVERHAMPTON**
Market Street and the Bilston Street Corner 1973 ZZZ03815 (Author's Collection)

This whole block of buildings was demolished to make way for the new Police Station opposite the Metro terminus. Similar well-built terraces of Victorian shops are now being restored, and the upper floors converted into apartments. The little gem of an early 18th-century house on the right remained unnoticed until it was too late.

WOLVERHAMPTON
Queen Street c1900
W285001

The west end of Queen Street joins Dudley Street here. This was one of the town's finest Georgian and Regency streets. E F Allen had a prestigious piano showroom but most of the shops are small premises which were demolished in the 1960s, including the Congregational Church of 1866. The far end still has most of the 18th-century buildings today, except for the Express & Star offices of the 1930s.

WOLVERHAMPTON, *Clifton Cinema, Bilston Street 1973* ZZZ03816 (Author's Collection)

The Clifton Cinema started as the Prince of Wales Theatre in 1863 on the site of a slaughter-house and went through various name changes including the Hippodrome and the New Theatre Royal. Rebuilt after a fire in 1913 it became a cinema in 1931 and was renamed the Clifton in 1948, ending its days as a bingo hall. It was demolished in 1978 to build the new Police Station - a sad loss to the store of interesting city buildings.

WOLVERHAMPTON
Snow Hill c1950
ZZZ03817 (Author's Collection)

The Swan and Peacock on the right was a half-timbered 17th-century coaching inn. The row of shops on the left was demolished to make way for the Wulfrun Centre in the 1960s. The Gaumont Cinema in the centre distance, opened in 1932, was the super-cinema of its day. In the 1960s and 1970s it was an established live rock music venue, where the Beatles played.

WOLVERHAMPTON, *Central Library, Snow Hill c1905* ZZZ03818 (Author's Collection)

A handsome brick and terracotta building designed by R T Hare, the Free Library opened in 1902. The inscription on the front indicates that it was built to commemorate the 60th year of Queen Victoria's reign in 1897. The area around the library has recently been designated the Learning Quarter and is featured as part of the city's improvement plans.

WOLVERHAMPTON
Victoria Street 1910
W285005

This was a major shopping street in 1910 with Cavit furnishers and Horace George the tailor, who had two shops in this street. The gables of the Star and Garter Hotel, a former coaching inn rebuilt in the 1830s and demolished in the 1960s, can be seen on the right. The dome of the Empire Palace Music Hall is in the centre distance.

▼ **WOLVERHAMPTON,** *Victoria Street c1955* W285308

In 1955 James Beattie's department store had a reputation for a high level of customer service and good quality merchandise that made it the best place to shop in town. Despite much competition the store still manages to retain this image. Burton's tailor shop on the right was taken over by Beatties, as it is now known, in 1992.

▶ **WOLVERHAMPTON**
Lindy Lou, Victoria Street 1973 ZZZ03819
(Author's Collection)

A plaque on the front dates Lindy Lou as 1300AD but in fact it is 17th-century. Originally the Hand Inn, it is best known to older inhabitants as Lindy Lou, a toy shop or the Copper Kettle, a teashop. It was stripped down to its wooden frame and refurbished in about 1980. Unfortunately although this probably rescued the building its ramshackle charm was lost.

WOLVERHAMPTON
*The View down
Victoria Street to
Penn 1975* ZZZ03820
(Author's Collection)

In the centre of the
picture is Beatties
department store. Then
it is possible to follow
the line of Victoria Street
and Worcester Street,
until the Penn Road dual
carriageway can be seen
almost on the horizon as
it rises to Goldthorn Hill.
The tower blocks of flats
at Graiseley were the first
high-rise flats to be built
in Wolverhampton.

► **WOLVERHAMPTON**
*The New Market
Hall c1965* W285056

The hall was officially
opened in 1960 when the
retail market was moved
from beside St Peter's
Church, now the site of
the present Civic Centre.
The market stalls were
originally to the left of
the new hall but have
now been moved and a
market square opened
up next to the Market
Hall, flanked by a block
of luxury city centre
apartments over shops.

WOLVERHAMPTON
Darlington Street 1890
W285003

Horse trams are slowly climbing the hill on their journey from Tettenhall. The shops on the left were demolished in the 1930s to make way for Burton Tailors and F W Bradford Ltd, a family-run department store incorporated into James Beattie in 1960. Stobart the tailors, on the right with the display of hats and caps, has now lost the corner of its ground floor.

WOLVERHAMPTON
Darlington Street c1905 ZZZ03821 (Author's Collection)

The Methodist Church was newly built in 1900. The shops to
its right were all demolished in the 1970s. Nothing has replaced
them so far except a car park, but a law court complex is planned
for the site. Bennett Clark by the YWCA on the left was a well-
known local photographer. The cart on the right is from Pelham
Laundry in Pelham Street.

WOLVERHAMPTON
Darlington Street c1955 W285307

Although dating from the 1950s this scene looks remarkably
similar today. Darlington Street is shorter now having lost its
bottom 100 yards to the new Chapel Ash traffic island in the 1960s.
The dome of the Methodist Church (1900) is visible on the left and
the spire of St Mark's Church (1849) still terminates the view west.

WOLVERHAMPTON
from the air 1937 AF53724BR

MOLINEUX AND THE SURROUNDING AREA

MOLINEUX HOUSE originally stood in North Street before the ring road cut the street in half. North Street had been a flourishing shopping street at the town end, and the area was home to thousands of people who lived in North Street, Molineux Street, Vincent Street, Dawson Street, Camp Street, Nursery Street and a whole network of others. Now all the houses and people have gone and the redevelopments of the Molineux football ground, the University and Asda have taken over much of the area.

So in a different way the area has regained its importance. Thousands of fans converge on Molineux on match days, and Asda is a very successful supermarket. The University has a large campus here north of the ring road and houses many of its students in the complex of hostels at Lomas Street and Randall Lines House.

The University also uses part of the Molineux Steve Bull Stand as offices.

WOLVERHAMPTON, *The Molineux Football Ground c1960* W285035
Since 1889 the home of Wolverhampton Wanderers, the stadium was formerly a pleasure park created in the 1860s in the grounds of Molineux House. There were gardens, a bandstand, a lake and an athletics track round a playing field. This is the Waterloo Road stand with the South Bank on the left.

The land where these houses were is now part of Molineux football ground. G O'Connor's on the corner did shoe repairs. A little further down at 109 North Street Mrs Doris Preece kept the family second-hand and factory surplus clothing shop. A suit from Mrs Preece was £5 and a pair of shoes only 75p in 1976. Her best customers were the Polytechnic students.

WOLVERHAMPTON, *Waterloo Road, The Molineux Football Ground 1978* ZZZ03823 (Author's Collection)

The Waterloo Road Stand was built in 1925 with dressing rooms below. The angle of the road gave it a kink in the middle. In the 1970s new crowd safety legislation forced the rebuilding of unsatisfactory parts of the ground. The rebuilt Waterloo Road Stand, now called the Billy Wright Stand, is the showpiece entrance to Molineux.

WOLVERHAMPTON
Molineux Street
1979 ZZZ03824 (Author's Collection)

This stand, built to hold a crowd of 8,000, was opened in 1932 just as Wolverhampton Wanderers returned to Division One. Although an all-seat stand, by the 1970s it would not pass the new safety legislation standards and it was rebuilt as the John Ireland Stand in 1979 to seat 9,500. Molineux Street itself and a large part of North Street were built over and the pitch was moved some way to the east.

THE WOLVES FA CUP-WINNING TEAM *1949* ZZZ03825 (Wolverhampton Wanderers Football Club Archives)

Wolves beat Leicester City 3-1 at Wembley on 30 April 1949. The line-up is back row: (left to right) Billy Crook, Roy Pritchard, Bert Williams, Bill Shorthouse, Terry Springthorpe. Front row: Johnny Hancocks, Sammy Smyth, Stan Cullis (manager), Billy Wright, Jesse Pye, Jimmy Dunn, Jimmy Mullen. Scorers for Wolves were Jesse Pye (2) and Sammy Smyth (1). A celebratory banquet was held at the Café Royal in London.

SIR JACK HAYWARD *2003* ZZZ03826 (Wolverhampton Wanderers Football Club Archives)

In May 2003 Wolves beat Sheffield United 3-0 to gain promotion to the Premier League. Here a very happy Sir Jack Hayward, owner and President of the club since 1990, proudly holds the Play-Off Championship Trophy.

THE STATUE OF BILLY WRIGHT ZZZ03828 (Wolverhampton Wanderers Football Club Archives)

Billy Wright, born in Ironbridge, Shropshire in 1924, was one of the greatest Wolves captains. He took over the captaincy in 1947 from Stan Cullis and led Wolves to the FA Cup Championship in 1949 and League Championships in 1958 and 1959. He won a total of 105 England caps. When he died in 1994 Sir Jack Hayward commissioned this statue, which was unveiled by his widow Joy Beverley in 1996.

BERT WILLIAMS
Legendary Wolves Goalkeeper ZZZ03827
(Wolverhampton Wanderers Football Club Archives)

Bert Williams was considered to be one of the best goalkeepers in the world in the early 1950s. He was born in Bradley, Bilston in 1922 and played 22 times for England. Here he is playing for England against Scotland at Hampden Park in 1950. He was nicknamed 'The Cat' by Italian football fans. Billy Wright is on the extreme left.

WOLVERHAMPTON, *The Molineux Hotel 1973* ZZZ03829 (Author's Collection)

After the gardens of Molineux House were sold off as a pleasure ground in the 1860s, Molineux Hotel prospered reasonably well until the 1970s when it was cut off from the town centre by the ring road and found itself perched on top of a concrete cliff with poor access. It closed in 1979 and remained empty and deteriorating for over twenty years.

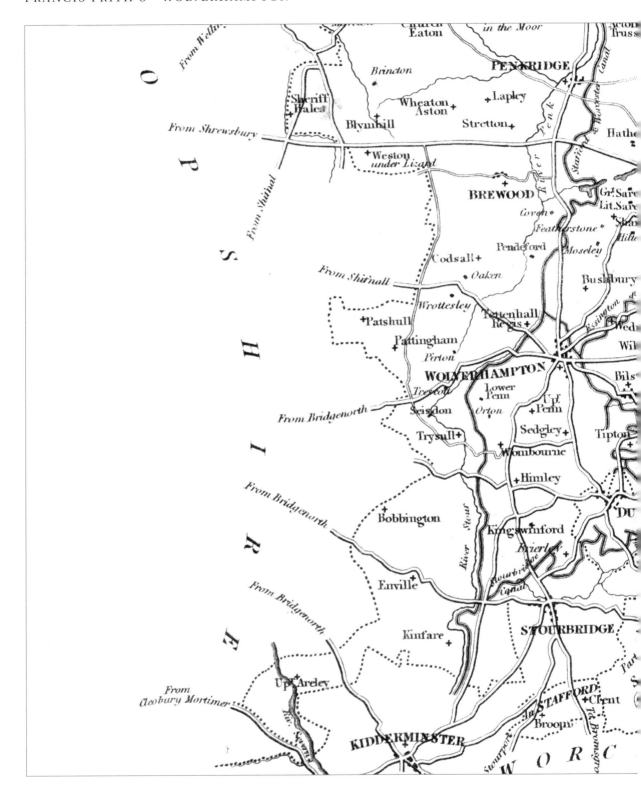

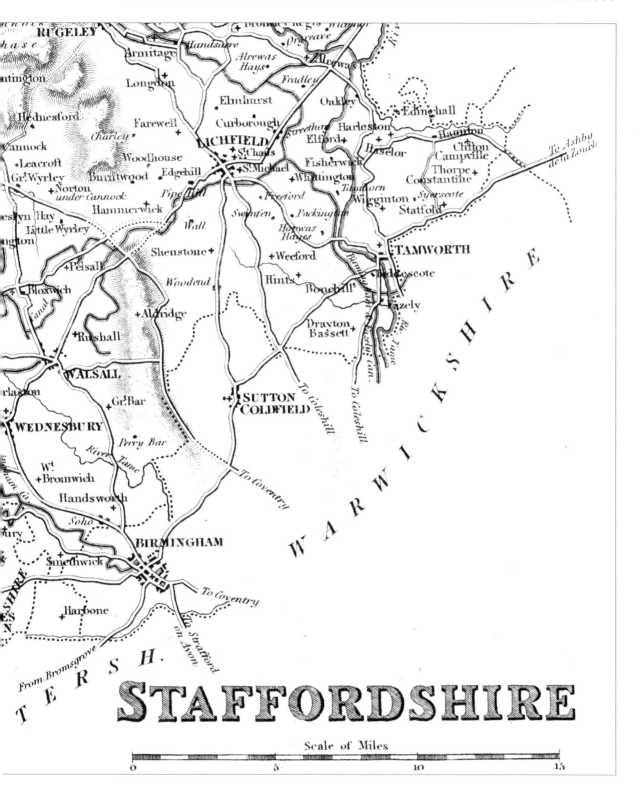

PENN AND THE SOUTH

THE ANCIENT VILLAGE of Penn could be much older than Wolverhampton, the town that eventually grew to engulf it. With a Celtic pre-Saxon name and a pre-Conquest Saxon church, Penn remained a small settlement for well over a thousand years. High on the hill and surrounded by farmland the village retained its rural atmosphere until the 1930s when the road from Wolverhampton became lined with houses as far as Spring Hill. The parish of Penn was very extensive including Upper and Lower Penn, Finchfield, Merry Hill and Bradmore.

The road from Wolverhampton to the south had been well built up by the 19th century for a mile or so out of town with a mixture of Victorian terraces and villas. After the First World War, the construction of houses for the middle classes continued the conversion of the former farming lands to housing estates. A large part of the area is still called Penn Fields.

WOLVERHAMPTON, *The Royal Wolverhampton School c1955* W285031

The Royal Wolverhampton School sits in a commanding position on Goldthorn Hill on the Penn Road outside the city centre, which has become dual carriageway to the Kidderminster Road, except for the mile that starts here and goes as far as Penn Village. This has caused the Victorian atmosphere of this section of the road to be preserved.

WOLVERHAMPTON
The Royal Wolverhampton School c1955
W285030

The Royal School began its life as an orphan asylum in the former Dispensary building in Queen Street. The 1849 cholera epidemic had left many orphans in the town. The Royal Orphanage moved to these buildings in Penn Road, which it still occupies, and became the Royal Wolverhampton School.

PENN, *The Cinema 1973* ZZZ03830 (Author's Collection)

Opened in Warstones Road in 1937, the Penn was a favourite suburban cinema with a huge local clientele who could walk there or easily park. It was a safe venue for children who attended its matinees until 1969. With the demise of traditional cinemas in the 1970s it was sold to developers who built a supermarket on the site.

◀ **PENN**
Spring Hill Corner
c1965 P157026

This parade of shops in Spring Hill now faces the dual carriageway on the southern edge of the city. The area was built up in the 1930s and the shops date from then. They look superficially the same today but the post office has closed, Colman's the grocer has become a Chinese take-away, and the hardware shop is now a car parts shop.

PENN
The Village c1965
P157022

Penn Road was a bottleneck so narrow in places that two buses could only pass with difficulty. The dual carriageway has taken away this problem but only at the expense of half of Penn village. Penn Road runs along a major underground geological fault line where the coal measures are and in one stretch the southbound lane is higher than the northbound lane.

PENN
Wolverhampton from Spring Hill Lane c1970
P157018

Spring Hill Lane runs from Warstones Road up the hill to Lower Penn and on to Dimmingsdale. It is a very desirable housing area and there are long views over the suburbs of Penn and Merry Hill to the wooded heights of Tettenhall and beyond. The new flats at Merry Hill were 'highly commended' in 1969 in the national 'Good Design in Housing' competition.

► **WOLVERHAMPTON**
Penn Common c1955
W285020

The common is still very much an important green space south of the city. The golf club has been using part of the common since 1892 and bought the title of Lord of the Manor in 1955 from the Duke of Sutherland. A deed of declaration in 1961 gave the public access to the land but forbade grazing unless farmers could produce evidence of ancient rights.

◀ WOLVERHAMPTON
Penn Common c1955
W285021

The Brewhouse, known as the Tower House, is believed to have formed part of the Earl of Dudley's estate. It was a good place for a brewery as the area was well supplied with spring water. It became a dwelling in about 1900 and was converted into two-bedroomed luxury apartments in 1974 selling for as much as £8000 each.

OUT TO THE WEST

TETTENHALL was another prosperous village of ancient foundation to the west of Wolverhampton dating from Anglo-Saxon times. A rural settlement serving the surrounding farmland, it lay on the main road from London to Holyhead. The old roads from Wolverhampton to Tettenhall and Compton through Chapel Ash were developed for housing from the early 19th century onwards. Towards Tettenhall particularly, there are still miles of handsome Victorian and Edwardian villas along the wide tree-lined road all the way down to Newbridge, where it crosses the canal.

Tettenhall itself retains its distinctive local shopping centre for the largely unspoiled village but it has now become a prosperous and desirable place to live for many people, who mostly work elsewhere during the day. Some of the most expensive housing in the city is in the Tettenhall area.

CHAPEL ASH *c1905* ZZZ03831 (Author's Collection)

The prominent building in the centre still stands at the divide between Compton Road on the left and Tettenhall Road on the right. Compton Road was lined with mature trees at this time. They died back over the years but some have recently been replaced at this end.

CHAPEL ASH
c1955 W285302

This is a tranquil scene no longer. The roads from Tettenhall, Compton and Bradmore converge here and funnel city centre traffic down this street. The Alexandra pub remains but the grocer, butcher, baker and fish shop of the 1960s have become estate agents, take-away food outlets and furniture shops. The housewife shops elsewhere for her daily supplies.

WOLVERHAMPTON, *The Grammar School c1960* W285038

Wolverhampton Grammar School was founded in 1512 by Sir Stephen Jenyns. It moved from early 18th-century premises in John Street to this building, on the rural edge of the town in 1875. The main building was designed by Giles and Gough of London in Early Tudor style. The metal railings have now been replaced in the original style.

**TETTENHALL
ROAD**
c1905 ZZZ03832
(Author's Collection)

The tram is making
its way back to
Wolverhampton from
Newbridge. Tettenhall
Road was widened and
improved by Thomas
Telford in the 1820s as
part of the London to
Holyhead Road, now the
A41. There was criticism
at the time that it was a
waste of money because
it was too wide. Not
many motorists would
say that now.

TETTENHALL, *The Church c1910* ZZZ03833 (Author's Collection)
The medieval parish church of St Michael was founded before the Domesday Book was compiled in 1086. Tettenhall was a
small village several miles into the country for most of its existence until the expansion of Wolverhampton engulfed it in the
19th century. It remained outside the town with its own council however until 1966.

TETTENHALL, *The Parish Church c1960* T140013a

The church was mysteriously burnt down in 1950. Fire appliances apparently had difficulty reaching the church buildings from the road. The only parts remaining after the fire were the 14th-century tower and the 19th-century porch. The nave was beautifully rebuilt in a new design by B Miller but in a sympathetic Gothic style.

► **TETTENHALL**
*The Post Office
and Upper Green*
c1965 T140012

Anyone who is
familiar with
Tettenhall village
today would be
astonished at the
lack of cars in this
scene. The Post
Office is still there,
and the butcher,
but Tettenhall is no
longer the sleepy
centre it once was.
Redevelopment
of shops has been
largely limited to one
side of High Street:
this corner of the
village stills retains its
old time feel.

◄ **TETTENHALL**
The Clock Tower
c1960 T140005

The landmark Clock
Tower on Upper Green
was built to celebrate
the coronation of King
George V in 1911. The
inscriptions read 'I labour
here with all my might
to tell the hours by day
and night' and 'For every
hour that comes there is
a hope'. It was the gift of
local landowners Mr and
Mrs E Swindley.

▲ **TETTENHALL,** *Upper Green c1965* T140060

This is still one of the most popular, and free, attractions for young children. It began its life as a farm pond before being turned into a safe paddling pool in about 1934. It was paid for by the Graham family, proprietors of the Express and Star, the local evening newspaper.

TETTENHALL
Wood Road and the Institute c1910 ZZZ03834
(Author's Collection)

Tettenhall Wood lies along the road from Tettenhall village to Perton and Pattingham. The Institute is still used as a community centre, but everything else here has gone. There are new shops just past the Institute on the right, and on the left corner, where there was a butchers shop, there are now flats.

▶ **TETTENHALL**
Old Hill c1900
ZZZ03835 (Author's
Collection)

The main road
through Tettenhall
village from
Wolverhampton
wound its way up
the steep sandstone
ridge and up to the
shops by Upper
Green until the 1820s.
It was a notorious
bottleneck relieved
by the turnpike trust,
which cut the present
road that bypasses
the village centre.
These were the days
when fresh bread was
delivered daily by
horse and cart.

◀ **WOLVERHAMPTON**
*Merridale Road
c1905* ZZZ03836
(Author's Collection)

This road was laid out
from the 1860s with
pleasant villas and
terraces. The town ended
just where this road
turns in the distance,
then there were just
farms, until Bradmore
village. Suburban
development soon
pushed the borders
miles further out into
the countryside. Most
gaps left were filled in
with housing between
the wars.

▲ **WOLVERHAMPTON,** *West Park, the Lake c1940* ZZZ03837 (Author's Collection)

Among the most popular activities in the park has always been hiring a rowing boat for an hour on the lake in the summer. The local belief was that the deepest water in the lake was so deep it would hide a double-decker bus. Nonetheless this has never deterred the rowers.

◄ **WOLVERHAMPTON**
*West Park, Flower Beds
c1911* ZZZ03838 (Author's Collection)

The local council has always made a special effort to maintain wonderful floral displays, despite a lack of other maintenance over the years. This is the view in 1911 of the mobile floral crown built by West Park gardeners to celebrate the coronation of George V.

► **WOLVERHAMPTON**
West Park c1960
W285044

The conservatory by the lake opened in 1896 and was fully restored in 1993/4. New supports were inserted inside to support the roof but without spoiling the Victorian design. It houses a fascinating collection of exotic hot-house plants. The boats for hire are drawn up along the bank nearby.

WOLVERHAMPTON
The Clock, West Park
c1965 W285058

One of the best examples of a Victorian park in the country, West Park was designed by H Vertegans and opened to the public in 1881 on the site of the town racecourse. The park is now being splendidly restored to its original plan and the buildings repaired. The clock was presented by a local councillor in 1883 and restored in 1991.

WEDNESFIELD, BILSTON AND THE EAST

WEDNESFIELD is one of the places, like Wednesbury, apparently named in early Anglo-Saxon times after the pagan god Woden, or Odin. A small settlement for centuries, it attracted large numbers of new inhabitants as it expanded from the 18th century onwards with the growth of industry in the area. It was absorbed into the borough of Wolverhampton in 1966.

Bilston also became part of Wolverhampton in 1966. Another old settlement, it dates from before the Norman Conquest. It was a pre-existing hamlet when the Domesday book was compiled in 1086. It was always a more prosperous local town than Wednesfield, but in the same way there was a vast increase in population when industry took over as the main economic activity.

WEDNESFIELD, *The Bowling Green c1965* W236007

Bowls is still a very popular pastime in the Midlands. Wednesfield Bowling Green is in the park, which was laid out in 1925. There were flower gardens and a paddling pool, and the George V playing fields were added just before the war. The flowers around the bowling green look like kniphofia or red-hot poker.

WEDNESFIELD, *High Street c1965* W236015

This is the High Street after it was widened, but before it was bypassed. The new shops on the left were built in 1959 behind the old shops, then the old ones were demolished. St Thomas's Church behind the trees was consecrated in 1750 and burned out in 1902. The lower part of the tower was retained in the rebuilt church.

WEDNESFIELD
The Canal and the Flats c1965 W236013

The coming of the canal in the 18th century opened Wednesfield up to industrialisation and brought in large numbers of new inhabitants, who had to be housed quickly and cheaply. These houses have been largely cleared away and tower blocks like this one built, which are now generally accepted to be a mistake and are themselves being replaced.

BILSTON *c1960* B353004

The Town Hall on the corner of Lichfield Street and Church Street was built in 1872 and was the home of Bilston Urban District Council until Bilston was incorporated into Wolverhampton in 1966. It gradually became unused and its condition deteriorated. It has now been reprieved and is used for community activities.

BILSTON, *St Leonard's Church c1960* B353023

Built in classical style in 1825-6, St Leonard's is one of the treasures of Bilston. The medieval church tower base was the only part not demolished. Its burial ground was the final resting-place of hundreds of cholera victims in 1832, until it could take no more and the graveyard of St Mary's Church and Swan Bank Methodist Church were used.

BILSTON
*The Greyhound and
Punchbowl Inn c1960*
B353005

Dating from the 15th
century this was the ancient
manor house of Stowheath.
It became a pub in 1829 and
was completely refurbished
in 1936. By the 1960s it
had fallen into disrepair
once more and recently
underwent a thorough
renovation. It is still in use
as a pub and there is a
finely carved overmantel
and an ornate Jacobean
plaster ceiling.

WOLVERHAMPTON
East Park c1955
W285017

To create East Park many trainloads of soil were brought in to cover a bare expanse of waste ground in Stowheath owned by the Duke of Cleveland. It was the second great public park created in Wolverhampton in 1895/6 after the West Park. Over the succeeding years the open land all round was filled in with housing estates.

WOLVERHAMPTON, *East Park c1955* W285019

The grounds of East Park were designed with assistance from Thomas Mawson, a landscape architect based in Cumbria. His name is not widely known now but he laid the foundations of modern landscape architecture. There had been a large lake in the park but the ground was riddled with mine workings and the leakages could not be stopped.

INDEX

NAMES OF PRE-PUBLICATION BUYERS

THE FOLLOWING PEOPLE HAVE KINDLY SUPPORTED THIS BOOK BY SUBSCRIBING TO COPIES BEFORE PUBLICATION.

James Christopher Allen, born 28 Dec 2002
Peter & Astra Aleksandrowicz
Andrea & Alex
Olive Arnold, Wolverhampton
In memory of William & Gladys Baker
Judy Banks just 'In memory'
Kathleen E Beddard
David & Dorothy Bennett, Wolverhampton
Billy Bond & Family, Wolverhampton
Joan Evelyn Bristo & Dennis Bristo
In memory of Mrs C J Broadfield,
    Wolverhampton
Mr & Mrs G W N Brown, Wolverhampton
Michael J Brown, Wolverhampton
Robert Brown, Birthday 1st May 2005
Denise June Burns (nee Holden)
Happy Birthday Chrissy, love Derek
Christine Clare, Wolverhampton
Marjory Clare, Wolverhampton
In memory of J M Clarke, Merry Hill
Janet & Roger Clowson
In memory of Kristian Constable of Penn
N L Cullis, I H Cullis, D G Cullis & DA Cullis
Danielle, Charlotte & James Cummings
Mrs M Cummings, Penn, Wolverhampton
Stan, Mary & Bob Darby
Sandy & Olly Darlington, Wolverhampton
The Davenport Family, Penn
John V Davies
Wallace Davies, Wolverhampton
In memory of Tommy Deadman, Speedway Ace
Carole Elizabeth Dean, Wolverhampton
Mr D Dodd, Wolverhampton, on his
    85th Birthday
As a tribute to my parents, George Dovey
E Dunn, Crete 1941 Fleet on Valiant Heart
Elizabeth Dunn, Wedding Congratulations 2005
In memory of Hazel Norah Edwards
Mr H T Ellis on his 60th Birthday
Keith Farley; Emma, Richard & Matthew
In memory of John Finch
Lynda Flavell, Penn, Wolverhampton

To Shaun from Nan Fletcher, Wolverhampton
Doreen Fullwood (nee Clare), Wolverhampton
The Galloway Family, Wolverhampton
Mr R & Mrs I Giddins, Merry Hill
Mr & Mrs L Gill
Fred Goodman, Wolverhampton
The Green Family, Wolverhampton
Harry Griffiths
In memory of Bernard & Brenda Hales
Douglas Harold Hall, 'Happy Birthday'
The Hancock Family, Wolverhampton
Robert Allen Harding, Wolverhampton
Anthony & Rhona Harris of Finchfield,
    Wolverhampton
The Harris Family, Finchfield, Wolverhampton
Mr S T & Mrs T A L Hewitt
Mr T P & Mrs P Hewitt
The Hindley Family, Wolverhampton
Pat & Bill Holt of Wolverhampton
Len & Cath Hooper
Norman F Horobin
Mrs J P Hurlstone, Shifnal
Mrs L Huse, Wolverhampton
Bert Illidge
Horace & Una Illidge
Stephen & Ann Illidge
Brian Jackson & The Jackson Family
Dave Jebb, Wolverhampton
Andrew & Rosa Jervis of Wolverhampton
In memory of Frances & Jack Jones,
    Wolverhampton
Josie & Mike
Kathleen & Roland, Penn, Wolverhampton
E H Kay, Wolverhampton
The Keates Family, Penn
Clive Edward Knowles, White Hall, Oswestry
Malcolm John Knowles, Harrington Hall,
    Bridgnorth
In memory of Tony Kokinis, Penn
David Gerald Lampitt & The Lampitt Family
For Derek Lawton from Di
The Lea Family (IRL), Wolverhampton

Leslie Leedham
Florence Doreen Lewis, Wolverhampton
Mr James George Marston, Wolverhampton
Mr A J & Mrs M B Mason, Wolverhampton
D C B Matthews MBE & Family, Penn
Dr & Mrs Graham Morley, Wolverhampton
The Morris Family, Penn, Wolverhampton
Margaret Morris, Wolverhampton
To Mervyn Morris on his 70th Birthday
Neil & Liz Morris, Wolverhampton
Mrs Stella Morris & Family
The Mott Family, Wolverhampton
The Nehru Family, Wolverhampton
Mr T A & Mrs B M Newill, Wolverhampton
Leslie A Nicholas, Wolverhampton
Nikki & Stuart, 15th Anniversary 30-06-05
To our son David Owen on his birthday,
    from Mom & Dad
Bev Parker, Wolverhampton
Mr M M Patel, Wolverhampton
Stephen Pearson, Wolverhampton
Mr Kevin Perks, Australia
David & Audrey Perry & Family, Penn
Len Phelps
Sue & Don Pickering, Pennfields
Sarah & Daryl Poultney
Frances Pountney
June I Radford & Family
Mr & Mrs C A Reade, Wolverhampton
Thomas G Reid, Penn, Wolverhampton
Michael Relves
June Richards
Mr Harold B Ricou, Wolverhampton
The Rogers Family, Wolverhampton
Rosamund Rostance, Wrington, Bristol
Mr & Mrs A Sadler
Mr J S Sadler & Mrs P E Sadler
In memory of Ernest Sadler of Coseley
Alan & Carol Schofield and children
Alex S B Sealey, Wolverhampton
Don Sharp, MBE, Penn, Wolverhampton
Ian Sharp, Penn, Wolverhampton

Mr J B & Mrs D M Simmonds, Wolverhampton
Stephen Michael Smith, Wolverhampton
Howard Stanley, Wolverhampton
Gary Stokes, Happy 40th, Wolverhampton
Rex M Thurstan, Wolverhampton
David Leslie Timmins, Morville, Bridgnorth
The Tonks Family, Wolverhampton
Mrs Doris Edna Towner & Mr George K Towner
A M Ware, Wolverhampton, formerly of Essex
Mrs G Wedge
The Wellsbury Family, Penn
In memory of F G Weston, Wolverhampton
Stuart White, Wolverhampton
Des & Marilyn Whitehouse, Lower Penn
Mrs E Whittaker & Family
John D Wilkes, Wolverhampton
The Williams Family, Ettingshall,
Wolverhampton
Margaret Wilson, Wolverhampton
Wolverhampton Chronicle
Mr & Mrs A Wood, Stourton
Heather & Steve Woodward, Wolverhampton
Mr D L Worwood, Wolverhampton
Mr G S Worwood, Ashton Keynes
The Wright Family, Wolverhampton
To Malcolm & Debbie Wright, Wolverhampton

FRITH PRODUCTS & SERVICES

Francis Frith would doubtless be pleased to know that the pioneering publishing venture he started in 1860 still continues today. Over a hundred and forty years later, The Francis Frith Collection continues in the same innovative tradition and is now one of the foremost publishers of vintage photographs in the world. Some of the current activities include:

Interior Decoration

Today Frith's photographs can be seen framed and as giant wall murals in thousands of pubs, restaurants, hotels, banks, retail stores and other public buildings throughout the country. In every case they enhance the unique local atmosphere of the places they depict and provide reminders of gentler days in an increasingly busy and frenetic world.

Product Promotions

Frith products are used by many major companies to promote the sales of their own products or to reinforce their own history and heritage. Frith promotions have been used by Hovis bread, Courage beers, Scots Porage Oats, Colman's mustard, Cadbury's foods, Mellow Birds coffee, Dunhill pipe tobacco, Guinness, and Bulmer's Cider.

Genealogy and Family History

As the interest in family history and roots grows world-wide, more and more people are turning to Frith's photographs of Great Britain for images of the towns, villages and streets where their ancestors lived; and, of course, photographs of the churches and chapels where their ancestors were christened, married and buried are an essential part of every genealogy tree and family album.

Frith Products

All Frith photographs are available Framed or just as Mounted Prints and Posters (size 23 x 16 inches). These may be ordered from the address below. From time to time other products - Address Books, Calendars, Table Mats, etc - are available.

The Internet

Already ninety thousand Frith photographs can be viewed and purchased on the internet through the Frith websites and a myriad of partner sites.

For more detailed information on Frith companies and products, look at these sites:

www.francisfrith.co.uk
www.francisfrith.com
(for North American visitors)

See the complete list of Frith Books at:

www.francisfrith.co.uk

This web site is regularly updated with the latest list of publications from The Francis Frith Collection. If you wish to buy books relating to another part of the country that your local bookshop does not stock, you may purchase on-line.

For further information, trade, or author enquiries please contact us at the address below:
The Francis Frith Collection, Frith's Barn, Teffont, Salisbury, Wiltshire, England SP3 5QP.
Tel: +44 (0)1722 716 376 Fax: +44 (0)1722 716 881   Email: sales@francisfrith.co.uk

See Frith books on the internet at www.francisfrith.co.uk

FREE PRINT OF YOUR CHOICE

Mounted Print
Overall size 14 x 11 inches (355 x 280mm)

Choose any Frith photograph in this book.
Simply complete the Voucher opposite and return it with your remittance for £2.25 (to cover postage and handling) and we will print the photograph of your choice in SEPIA (size 11 x 8 inches) and supply it in a cream mount with a burgundy rule line (overall size 14 x 11 inches).
Please note: photographs with a reference number starting with a "Z" are not Frith photographs and cannot be supplied under this offer.
Offer valid for delivery to one UK address only.

PLUS: **Order additional Mounted Prints at HALF PRICE - £7.49 each** (normally £14.99)
If you would like to order more Frith prints from this book, possibly as gifts for friends and family, you can buy them at half price (with no additional postage and handling costs).

PLUS: **Have your Mounted Prints framed**
For an extra £14.95 per print you can have your mounted print(s) framed in an elegant polished wood and gilt moulding, overall size 16 x 13 inches (no additional postage and handling required).

IMPORTANT!

These special prices are only available if you use this form to order . You must use the ORIGINAL VOUCHER on this page (no copies permitted). We can only despatch to one UK address. This offer cannot be combined with any other offer.

Send completed Voucher form to:
The Francis Frith Collection, Frith's Barn, Teffont, Salisbury, Wiltshire SP3 5QP

 **Voucher** *for FREE and Reduced Price Frith Prints*

Please do not photocopy this voucher. Only the original is valid, so please fill it in, cut it out and return it to us with your order.

Picture ref no	Page no	Qty	Mounted @ £7.49	Framed + £14.95	Total Cost £
		1	Free of charge*	£	£
			£7.49	£	£
			£7.49	£	£
			£7.49	£	£
			£7.49	£	£
			£7.49	£	£

Please allow 28 days for delivery.
Offer available to one UK address only

* Post & handling	£2.25
Total Order Cost	£

Title of this book . . . .
I enclose a cheque/postal order for £ . . . .
made payable to 'The Francis Frith Collection'

OR please debit my Mastercard / Visa / Maestro / Amex card, details below

Card Number

Issue No (Maestro only)   Valid from (Maestro)

Expires   Signature

Name Mr/Mrs/Ms . . . .
Address . . . .
. . . .
. . . .
. . . . Postcode . . . .
Daytime Tel No . . . .
Email . . . .

ISBN 1-85937-970-2   Valid to 31/12/07

Would you like to find out more about Francis Frith?

We have recently recruited some entertaining speakers who are happy to visit local groups, clubs and societies to give an illustrated talk documenting Frith's travels and photographs. If you are a member of such a group and are interested in hosting a presentation, we would love to hear from you.

Our speakers bring with them a small selection of our local town and county books, together with sample prints. They are happy to take orders. A small proportion of the order value is donated to the group who have hosted the presentation. The talks are therefore an excellent way of fundraising for small groups and societies.

Can you help us with information about any of the Frith photographs in this book?

We are gradually compiling an historical record for each of the photographs in the Frith archive. It is always fascinating to find out the names of the people shown in the pictures, as well as insights into the shops, buildings and other features depicted.

If you recognize anyone in the photographs in this book, or if you have information not already included in the author's caption, do let us know. We would love to hear from you, and will try to publish it in future books or articles.

Our production team

Frith books are produced by a small dedicated team at offices in the converted Grade II listed 18th-century barn at Teffont near Salisbury, illustrated above. Most have worked with the Frith Collection for many years. All have in common one quality: they have a passion for the Frith Collection. The team is constantly expanding, but currently includes:

Paul Baron, Jason Buck, John Buck, Ruth Butler, Heather Crisp, David Davies, Louis du Mont, Isobel Hall, Lucy Hart, Julian Hight, Peter Horne, James Kinnear, Karen Kinnear, Tina Leary, Stuart Login, Sue Molloy, Glenda Morgan, Wayne Morgan, Sarah Roberts, Kate Rotondetto, Dean Scource, Eliza Sackett, Terence Sackett, Sandra Sampson, Adrian Sanders, Sandra Sanger, Julia Skinner, Miles Smith, Lewis Taylor, Shelley Tolcher, Lorraine Tuck, Miranda Tunniclisse, David Turner, Amanita Wainwright and Ricky Williams.